A Magical Gift

To:

From:

Personal Notes

The First Note

The magical gift
of
unconditional
love

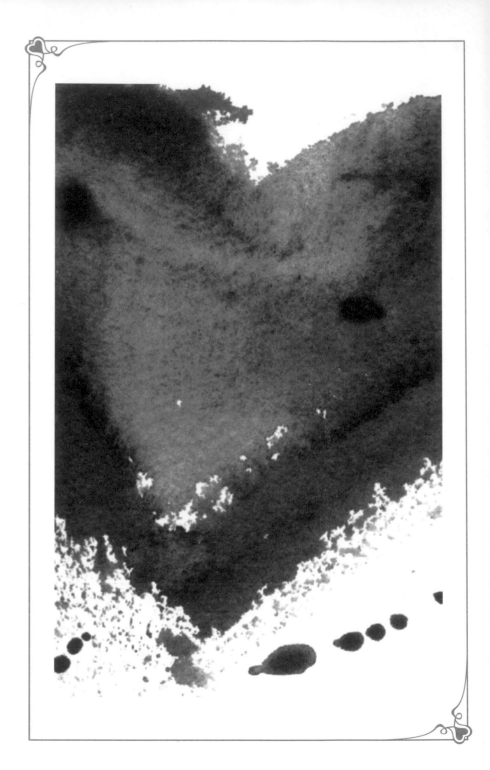

The First Note

The magical gift
of
unconditional
love

Joy Tsuya Joslyn & Don Joslyn

Art Farm Productions
Coloma, California

∞ This symbol is the trademark for
Art Farm Production's material concerning unconditional love.

Art Farm Productions • P.O. Box 457 • Coloma, California 95613

We retain the right to amend The First Note, as we grow in our
understanding of unconditional love.

First Printing, 1995
10 9 8 7 6 5 4 3 2 1

The First Note: The magical gift of unconditional love.
ISBN 0-9645259-0-9

Printed in the United States of America
for the people of the world.

We ask you to gently catch and release this gift in appropriate
waters if its message will benefit another.

A portion of the proceeds generated by the gift of this book will be
used to further the creative and humanitarian goals supported by
Art Farm Productions.

P.S. All double entendres intended.

Our Gift List
a small sampling

Spencer, our son
Gena, our daughter
Roy & Wuta; C.D. & Yvonne, our parents
Bryan, Paula
April, Toyo, Roland, Rikio, Mike, David, Jacqueline, Ben
Britt, Tolliver, Eileen, Alan, Robert, John, Larry

Lindsey, Oliver, Alysia, Danny, Amber, Becky, Bob, Carolynne, Chiye, Donna, Joan, Jack, David, Greg, Gretchen, Jennifer, Avis, Glenn, Norman, Janet, Jim, Joe, Ray, Joslyn, Lea, Korki, Ken, Mary Jane, May, Mitzie, Ted, Don, Clarke, Hawk, Deanna, Kim, Joel, Scott, Jimmy, Liane, Carlin, Taylor, Ardyth, Mark, Toshi, Veda, Mercyl, Melba, Carla, Mike, Barry, Stephen, Darlene, Jeff, Forrest, Susan, Deon, Fritz, Seun, Lois, Robert, Kearin, Venda, Cathy, Bruce, Matsuye, Misayo, Seichi, Hede, Jean, Rick, Art, Bonnie, Edith, Gary, Celia, Diane, Judy, Jon, Sister Mary Carlo, Elaine, Erinn, Anna Lee, Ling, Gabor, Manny, Maree, Barbara, Alieen, Gordon, Carol, Sumi, Tom, Swede, Wayne, Yaming, Ying, Walt, Ruth, Shannon, Heather, Lee, Norma, Camden, Karen, Kathleen, Lolly, Leo, Lani, Peter, Ash, Richard, Ron, Ed, Bill, Chuck, Sharon, Allen, Ann Marie, Li Syau, Joseph, Paul, Erica, Nettie, Sue, Dennis, Glenna, Carmy, Jo, Bridgett, Laurie, Steve, Marsha, Cynda, Cynthia, Jerry, Margie, Clyde, Stephanie, Marsh, Carl, Chris, Gil, Rachel, Gerry, Andy, Pat, Colin, Nancy, Jason, Devonne, Billie, Lura, Jay, Frank, Lynn, Alex, Karin, Lillian, Linda, Georgia, Nori, Valerie, Darrell, Carolyn, Rob, Wendy, Maria, Kay, Anna, Helayna, Helen, Veronica, Florence, Millie, Kikue, Charles, Ann, Randy, Larry, Dorine, Terry, Dale, Alan, Eric, Ola, Stewart, Brian, Kristen, Clint, Cheryl, Gene, J.D., Jan, Mandy, Mae, Sterling, Tola, Lucille, Maurice, Nick, Yvonne, Esther, Denise, Lorene, Anthony, John, Enid, Powell, Son, Kris, Doug, Loretta, Marika, Michele, Leon, Leno, Ingrid, Jackie, Booker, Mary, Warren, Pickard, Debbie, Al, EKG, Mona, Rochelle, Joyce, Kristie, Kathryn, Lilly, Roger, Shisue, Page, Suzanne, Muriel, Miyeko, Fred, and on and on
and on...

and the easiest of all, our grandsons,
Tyler and Cody

Unconditional
love
is
the
main
clue
in
the
Game
of
Life

Prologue

Each individual has to find
his or her own way -
learning many of life's lessons
by stumbling onto them
or by gleaning knowledge
from the experiences of others.

This book and its message
are a gift to you;
a gift from you to your children,
family, friends, and life partners
and especially from you to yourself.

It is a gift to all you love
and...

Introduction

We named this book The First Note
because this is the first opportunity
we have taken to write a
Note to all and
because love is truly the
first note in the Song of the Universe.

An intricate string of questions led us to
an answer of giving unconditional
love to our children. Fear and the
uncertainty of what we were going to
do almost stopped us. We had so
many questions and insecurities.

Knowing we will always love our children,
we are finding the
answers and the courage.

"Where to begin?"
With Love.

"What to say?"
Whatever it takes to make them understand.

"What to include?"
Everything.

"What to exclude?"
Fear, negative words, and sermons.

Is the timing right?"
Always.

"Maybe it isn't important, why bother?"

*All things need unconditional love
and will continually seek it.*

The eternal search can end.

*We are coming to terms with
unconditional love.*

*We have sufficient understanding of
unconditional love to let it become
the gift it was meant to be.*

*We are finding a way,
our own individual way.*

*It will continue to be a lifetime of
challenges and exciting possibilities.*

It is truly worth the effort.

Teaching our children and each other
that we love one another unconditionally
began
the unfolding of an incredible odyssey.

The experience is enlightening.
We are astonished that there is only
oppressive fear to relinquish and precious
freedom to gain.

Our attitudes about so many things are
changing. The world is a kinder place, and we
grow more accepting and content with
others and ourselves.

What euphoria to share
unconditional love!

We have been intrigued by the
expression: "The only true gift
is the gift of one's self."

What would a true gift encompass?
What true gift could we possibly ever give?

After we realized the impact of what
was happening in our lives, we had to
share the experience. It soon became
an obsession to tell anyone
who would listen.

Finally, we realized that unconditional
love was the gift we had been searching
for, for it is truly the gift of one's self.

Joy Tsuya Joslyn
Don Joslyn
Coloma, California
March 1995

The First Note

The magical gift
of
unconditional
love

There
is
magic
in
Love

Love
brings
spring
to
hibernating
spirits

Love
is a
tickle
that puts
a smile
in
life's
journey

Love
is
the rhythm
for the
Music
of your
Soul

Love
is the
first note
in the
Song
of
the
Universe

Many fairy tales and stories revolve around love, the necessity of being loved, finding love, and giving love.

Many a self-centered young prince has been given one last chance to know love by exchanging a seemingly insignificant kindness for the gift of love magically hidden in a humble trinket.

If the prince agreed, the magic trinket had the power to make his life complete; if the opportunity was rejected, the prince was made to live in the image of an animal or a revolting beast.

Once the prince rejected the opportunity, he had to reorganize his personal principles and priorities in order to be a man and receive the wonderful gifts that awaited him.

He had to learn to give of himself, embrace others, and understand, accept, and even laugh at himself so he could be free to experience love.

In reality, each individual is given
the opportunity to acquire the
magic trinket many times.

However, many individuals,
both women and men
of all ages, races, religions
and backgrounds, have allowed
themselves to become beasts by
denying themselves love in any of
its unique forms.

It is very painful to accept the fact
that learning to love
is something that needs one's own
intimate nurturing.

Some of life's goals
are to relinquish the fear,
honor the opportunity,
and win
the magic trinket.

The initial tidal wave of a new love
destroys the emotional wall of
protection that we have built
around ourselves.

Being creatures
with a strong instinct for survival,
we immediately find reasons and
excuses to rebuild the wall.

Brick by brick, soon the wall
is protecting us again from
the cacophony of life.

The bricks are made of insecurity,
deception, selfishness, and
hopelessness.

Fear is the mortar that holds the wall together.

The wall is our protection of choice from the pain of fear, rejection, guilt, and ridicule.

The wall is so strong it absorbs all emotions on both sides and blocks any music from either entering or leaving, making it impossible to hear or contribute to the Song of the Universe.

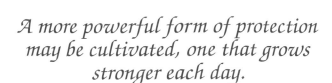

A more powerful form of protection
may be cultivated, one that grows
stronger each day.

This protection will help you understand
the fear and accept all life's challenges.

It will allow you to hear and enjoy the
positive music while it enhances your life
and the lives around you.

Its elements are personal dignity,
respect, integrity, courage, and wisdom.

The catalyst of laughter
begins strengthening the bond and
excelerating the process.

Its mortar is love, the love that
gives life and survives any onslaught.

That mortar, that love, is
unconditional love.

Unconditional love
bestows freedom,
freedom from
the pain
of fear,
deception,
and
rejection.

We all need to be loved -
loved unconditionally.

Actually giving
unconditional love is complex
and riddled with fear.

Embracing unconditional love
will force an understanding
and reorganization of
personal principles and priorities.

However, if the end goal is peace
and happiness for you and the ones
you love, then your efforts and
courage are worthwhile.

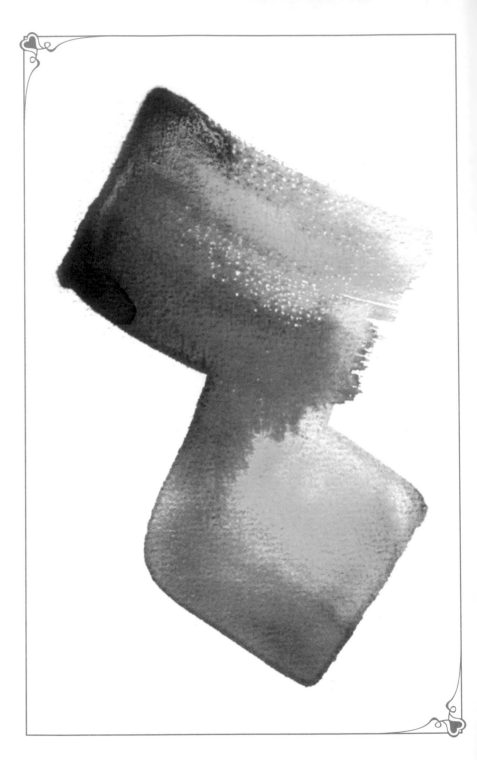

*The first step
toward receiving
personal
unconditional love
is learning
how to
love
another
unconditionally.*

Let

yourself

love

unconditionally.

*Start with the person
you feel most
in tune with.*

*Come to know
with all your heart
you love and
accept
that person.*

Tell

him

or

her

face

to

face.

As
your energy
and
courage
come through,
you begin
to share
in the
symphony
of
life.

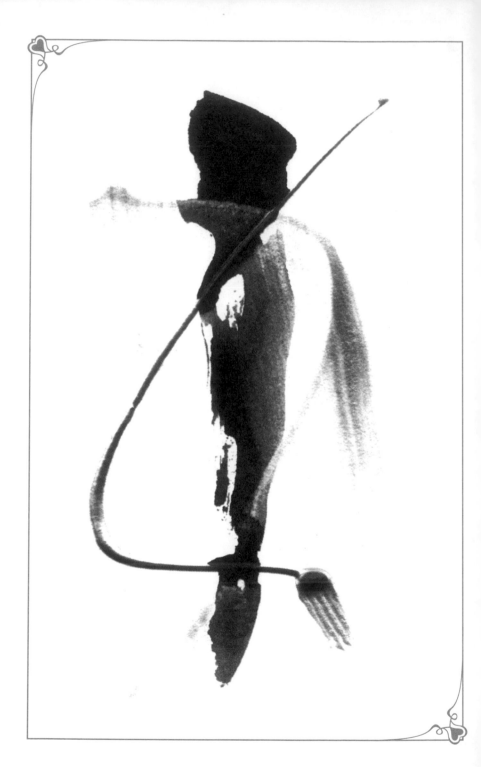

Giving
unconditional love
to
another
can create
a magical spell
to glisten
over
your
life.

The

spell

gives

you

the

freedom

to

be.

The
spell
affirms
your courage
and your gift.

It
summons
the orchestra
to
accompany
your aria.

*Then the
wonders
of the
spell
spill over
into an
acceptance
of yourself
and of
your
world.*

Now
you
can be
anything,
everything,
until finally
you are
the truly
happy
individual
you were
meant
to
be.

When you can honestly
say the following words,
you have started
down the path
of unconditional love,
and
the magical spell
will open
your heart
to the
Song
of
the
Universe:

"I

love

you

unconditionally.

My heart's desire

is for you

to be happy

and to

find and play

the

Music of your Soul,

so when your time

on earth

has ended,

you

can leave

with no regrets.

I love you

because

you have

the courage

to perform

your music

and to encourage me

as I compose

mine.

I

am always

with you

as you

struggle with

and

make peace

with your

life's challenges.

I
am proud
to be with you
and to share
in your
happiness
as you achieve
your goals
and live
your life
to
its
fullest.

I
continue
to love you
whether
we make contact
every day,
once a month,
or
once in a while.

I

encourage

you

to

discover

and

follow

your

bliss.

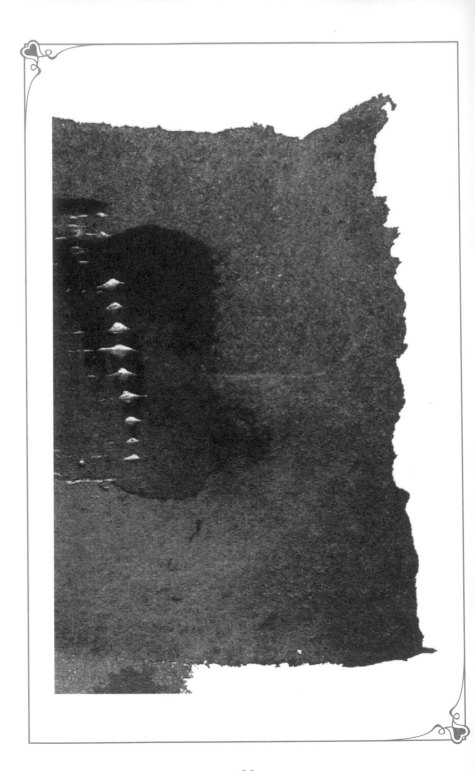

I
understand,

support,

and accept

that you

write

your own

composition

and

live within

your own

harmony.

Find

your own way

and learn

the lessons

brought

by

each

decision

you make.

It is

imperative

to

reap the benefits

and

learn

from your choices.

Now

accept

and

build upon

what ensues.

If I solve

your problem

my way,

I have taken away

the opportunity

for you to learn

your own way.

Your choice

was then

for naught.

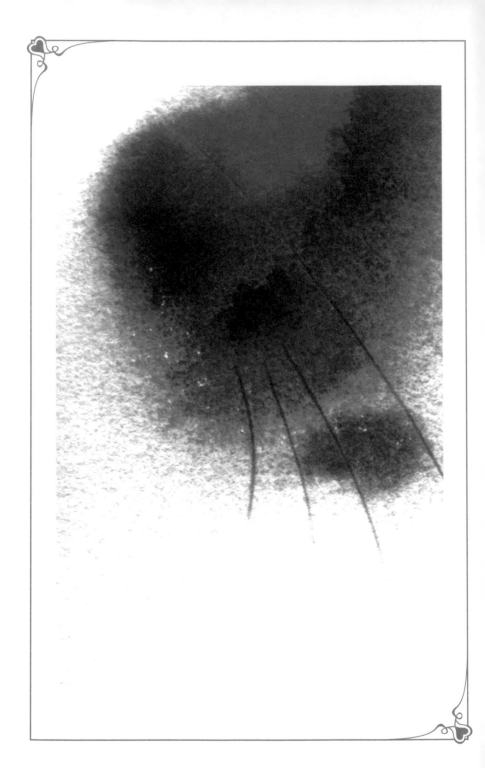

I

respect

all

your

choices.

.

I

relinquish,

expressed

or unexpressed,

control

over

your

thoughts,

actions,

and

beliefs.

The
joyful
laughter
in your
Music
makes me
smile
as
I
include
your life partners
in the love
I
have
for you.

I

accept

your

personal habits

and the way

you choose

to adorn

your

body.

I

respect

whatever

education

or

profession

you have

chosen.

I

honor

how you

support

your

personal

beliefs

in

religion

and

politics.

I

accept

your

sexuality

and

preference.

I

am

continually

delighted

by

your

growth

and

change.

Life is a
thrilling adventure
and you are
the conductor
of yours.
You are the one
who chooses,
organizes,
and lives
your adventure.
It can only
be as fascinating
as you make it.

I
acknowledge
your
efforts
to enhance
your
adventure
as
you
orchestrate
the
complexities
of
your journey.

I
support you
as you develop
the
unique talents
and
special abilities
necessary
for
your
adventure.

I
encourage you
to don
your Music
with care,

so
I may share
in your
discoveries
and
adventures
for many rich
and enchanting
years to come.

You
alone
are
responsible
for
the
outcome
of
your
adventure.

I love you;

therefore,

I will warn you

of any dangers

I perceive.

However,

you will have to make

your own choices

and live with

all the rewards

and consequences.

While
learning
to love yourself,
be open-minded
and
kind to others.

As you begin loving yourself,
begin to
"Do unto others
as you
would have them
do
unto
you."

Be a Prudent Adventurer

Being a prudent

adventurer

will allow you

to sample

the widest array

of

intriguing

odysseys.

Try New Things

Trying the
new and different
will open your life
to the
miracle of discovery
and the
delightful cymbalic awakening
of
who you are,
what you like,
what you don't like,
and how you want
to spend
your time
and
energy.

Enjoy All You Have

Enjoying all you have

will allow you

to happily

work towards making

all

your dreams

come

true.

Be willing to admit
you made a ~~mistake~~
                    poor choice

There are
no
mistakes
only
choices.

Recognizing
you
made
a poor choice
will free you
to move on
to another
ballad
or score.

*Listen
To Your Heart*

Learn to recognize

when it is time

to complete

a

journey

or

to begin

a new

adventure.

I want you
to have
exhilarating dreams,
to pursue
those dreams,
and to
realize
their
completion.

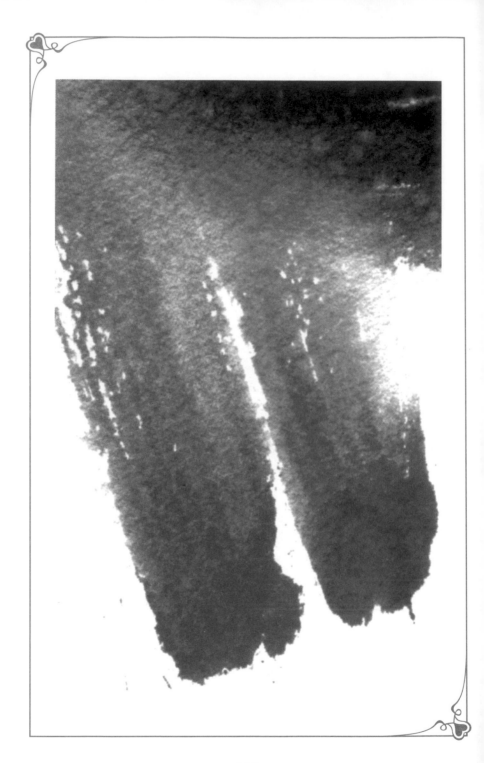

I want you

to discover

the

Music

of your

Soul

and combine it

with the

Song

of

the

Universe.

The

Choices

Are

Yours.

I

Want

You

To

Be

Happy!"

Epilogue

This book is a guide to help you
meet the challenge of learning how
to love unconditionally.

The process has the potential to:

1

Bring love and acceptance of yourself
and your world into your life.

2

Help you accept each individual's
need to grow, make choices,
learn from those choices,
and go on.

3

Help you forgive yourself and others.

The miracle of human existence is
the continual growth of one's spirit
and intellect and the constant need
to discover, learn, and develop
exciting new interests.

The uniqueness of an individual, as
it is being explored and developed,
is something to treasure.

It is impossible to force anything
into being a part of a relationship.
Each integral part must value the
gifts that are given so they may be
shared. A relationship can only
be nourished from a gift of
unconditional love when there is
mutual respect and appreciation.

Our Three Wishes

1
We wish for an exhilarating and peaceful world cared for by loving, happy, healthy individuals.

2
We wish leaders of militaries and militant organizations and their fellow soldiers be given the gifts contained in The First Note, *so ALL energies may be directed towards peaceful endeavors.*

3
We wish the individuals listed below may know unconditional love so their lives and the lives they touch may join in the Song of the Universe.

*Leaders of all
nations, people, and religions*

Managers of Industry

*Educators
Judges, Attorneys
Law enforcement agents*

*Newscasters, Writers
Athletes, Entertainers*

*Fathers, Mothers
Children*

*All you love
and...*

Acknowledgments

The First Note has been enriched
by the sensitivity of inspired people.

We are truly thankful to:

Yvonne & C.D. "Dick" Joslyn
for making this gift possible.

_All teachers, coaches,
doctors, nurses, and health care givers._

Roy I. Tsuya
Wuta Terazawa Tsuya
Spencer Fujimoto
Gena Joslyn
April Bosworth
Mike Bosworth
Toyo Tsuya Kahane
Ricky Rikio Tsuya
Peter Finn
Ash Fox
Lorene Mark
Lynn Pollock Marsh
Karin Marsh Reilly
Tolliver Swallow
Judy Shaffer
Carolyn Zerboni
Maree Layton Karrasch
David Hadley

Special appreciation is due an
extraordinary friend who made
The First Note sing.

Carolynne Gamble

The First Note

The magical gift of unconditional love

Joy Tsuya Joslyn & Don Joslyn

For additional books contact:
Art Farm Productions
P.O. Box 457 • Coloma, California 95613
Voice: 916-621-1340 • Facsimile: 916-621-0272

The
Beginning